MEN WOMEN
DOGS FLOWERS
CHOCOLATE
TRAVEL DEATH
LOVE MADNESS
TRADITION SEX
DRAGONS

Copyright © 2016, 2024 by Joe

Men Women Dogs Flowers Chocolate Travel
Death Love Madness Tradition Sex Dragons

REVISED EDITION

dontkilljoe.com

pub	1
cave	3
current events	4
catch-22	6
door	7
observation	8
desk	9
elephant	10
novel	11
making love	12
terror	13
revelation	14
avant garde	16
blue	17
comfort	18
countdown	19
seeds	20
field notes	21
drum	22
walking	23
noir	24
short story	26
relativity	27
angel	28
advice	29

science	30
deep time	31
ocean	32
estuary	33
range	34
joy	35
genesis	36
phillips	37
almonds	38
candle	40
priorities	41
echo	42
creatures	43
exceptional	45
quiet	46
childhood	48
diana	50
goose	51
daughter	52
birthday	54
vocabulary	55
poem	56
speech	57

My birth I can hardly remember.

EUGENE HÜTZ

feeling only—all I have to do is think it.

NORMA JEAN

Warning: *French*

I'm at the Irish pub

again, and I brought
Rimbaud, and he's

sixteen showing me
the dark room

of truth. He says:
Nous sommes à sec

d'amour. I say:
We can do better

than want—
we can give in.

This is not a poem.
C'est moi au-delà

des complies, breathing
like a drum.

I am a fish
in the black throat

of your dreams.
Don't pretend I know

what's happening.
This is not a poem.

*C'est le mot qui tombe
en morceaux*, like rain.

cave

Little golden crystal lights
but mostly it is dark.

Winter's endless silver nights
but mostly it is dark.

Sounds and electricity
but mostly it is dark.

Animals and history
but mostly it is dark.

current events

A friend of mine
once remarked
that my handwriting,

which leans left,
as if a wind
were blowing from

east of the page,
suggests that I
am an introvert.

People don't like
imagining what
an introverted guy

gets up to
any more than
they like

watching a woman
run for president.
It shouldn't hurt

this bad.
But it does. And
there's work to do.

catch-22

The law tells
us how to live. We
often break it.

Art shows us
how to live. We often
break it open.

door

after Martín Prechtel

In some languages
there is no word for
door, only mouth.

In some languages
there is no word for
blue, only sky.

And in yet
another language, spoken by few,
the word for

eye is bird
and light is a wing
in the dark.

observation

A window is
a door but more dangerous
to walk through.

a red desk

after Gaston Bachelard

Where it was come from is where it belongs and
isn't going to sing without you. Go now to the black
stove and flame the watch and crawl the papers
into punch after punch at the sky with its great
blue stomach. Believe the brown chairs when they
sit and refuse to put on their leggings. Also the
stairs believe them inasmuch as the trees are full
of wind. And should a stool tell you stories know
all the stories a lamp could also know how to tell
in the dark and on the floor of all the world in all
its hunger. The fan is watching. The walls lecture
per usual. The bricks lift up their dust from the
foundations of a small built life lumbering. So
give a roof its due. And don't forget to color the
nothings. It's winter and in love outside.

elephant

after Jack Gilbert

The world is no model house
like the womb is no simple bliss
and this is no daydream.

There is always somebody struggling to breathe
always light rotting in the vacuum
of our throats.

The good news
is that anything you choose to do
counts as work.

The good news
is that nobody really knows
how to fall asleep.

novel

for Will

In the beginning was the Turd
and the Turd was with Sod
and the Turd was Sod

making love

after Lawrence Durrell

Sometime in the middle of the night, I drew the curtains and fell asleep in a Cretan labyrinth to the crinkling sound of a minotaur's broken heart. After that, I put on my mask and liberated California with my sword, my horse, and my vigorous paramour. Finally, at half-past four I folded cheap American cheese into an egg pancake, lit two candles, and watched the light like sweat roll down the rosy cheeks of dawn.

terror

Maybe God is a wheel.
And fear is the rim.
And love is the hub.
And we are the spokes.

revelation

It begins
without
you.

(It begins
before
color.)

Then a
phrase, a
fraction of

breath,
some good
gods.

And walking
through
the air,

fastened to
Earth
like a bubble

you want
more, invent
less.

You get
the feeling
that Pilate

was afraid of
heights.
That

what we
take
takes us

home.
How do you
want to go?

Me?
I want to go
heaving.

avant garde

a mote a humming quiet snow

blue

The smell of the stairs
and that plastic bag
is all you need to know
about the backyard
unless of course you
are a human
in which case you should
probably be asleep.

comfort

> The wood whistles to heaven.
> Fire beats the air like a drum.
> It warms as I walk upstairs.
> Where the hell are my slippers?

countdown

I have been
waiting
for these legs
to know this earth
like wood.

I have been
outside
this body
with nothing
but words.

I have been
holding
your name
in my mouth
like smoke.

I have been
wanting
to use these
hands
for good.

seeds

after Jack Collom

The seeds fall
from the feeder like scales
on the piano.

A wren is
responsible for the symphony. Ode
to Early Autumn.

It would be
wise to write poems like
that—without starving.

It's not like
I cannot find ways to
feed and fill.

It's about the
swinging bell of my gut
dancing with time.

The wren looks
at me sideways then leaps
off into space.

field notes

I have detected
extremely superstitious behavior
especially as regards
the placement of marks
on paper.
They like to put numbers
in the corners
and count them.

drum

        hollow hollow hello
        halo hallow hallow halo hello
        hello hallow hollow

walking the dog on a cool evening

after Robert Frost

I watch the way the pines are tall.
They reach into the blue of day.
They reach above all other things.
I walk the dog the normal way.

The pines are tall as if to say
"You walk around and someday die
Whereas we stand here tall and true
And keep the birds and kiss the sky."

I watch the way the pines are right.
They reach into the black of night.
They reach above my dog and I
And keep the birds and kiss the sky.

noir

> I wander the long loop
> at night's end, trying to see.
>
> There, over there, stands
> a shadow, my shadow
>
> with a feather in his cap.
> Where have you been
>
> my dear, my noisy breath
> my face? It is so quiet
>
> in the thick without
> your heat. Cover me
>
> with your blanket bones
> your soot and your
>
> mumbles. Clothe me
> in oil, rub me with salt,
>
> make me ring. I am
> the bell of know-not.

I blush golden flakes.
And you, and your

expectations—you
run red, and you love.

short story

> DiFenestra was a man
> you couldn't trust
> around windows.

relativity

There's plans to land on the moon
and there's a backyard barbecue.

I trust the gravity that
holds us together: you and me

and the room. The tide of
a small space recalls the sea.

That we should want in order to
fill, that we should fill in order to

spend. The birds are quiet
this morning. The ground is wet.

The trees are fast asleep.
Dreaming leaves.

I once was an angel

after Apollo 11

> But that was yesterday and now we are
> so far we are so many million beats and
> the tempo is lightless and we are all eyes.
> And what of trust where there's dust is
> there trust? I keep words in my mouth
> like eggs. Where they start is the heart's
> business you know this I know. But which
> heart? There is the one there are the
> many the matter there is is that are has
> no single thing. How is a heart so near
> and so nowhere? At which circle will
> hours be silent?

advice

keep an egg in your dream
and a shadow in your mouth

science

>We found the moon. It was
>in an alley downtown 'round about
>
>midnight, weeping for America.
>
>And we all got to sobbing
>and the oceans rose up to our
>
>ankles.

deep time

Everybody has a little stone
in their chest.

The stone is a stone
if you're working or at rest.

There is no special science no
device by which to test

the special reason for there being
little stones in all our chests.

ocean

How proud I am to know these words
To walk this bridge on my lips

I wade into the wash of your voice
Like dust into the butterlight

And crumble in the heat
Of the downing molten sun

A human idea shivers
Beyond the skull

A stone sleeps in the surf
Sweating sand breathing bone

estuary

The lamp stalks the page
like a heron.

Little fish in
the shadow of rapture.

Salvation
ripples.

range

>You could say
>the poem comes
>the way the weather do
>and the poet is the first cow
>to lie down.

ode to joy

Tears are

maybe color
in love.

Maybe color
devastated.

Maybe mountains.

genesis

And God said
Let there be names.

And man grew accustomed
to the sense of himself.

And nobody knew
what to do about that.

phillips

fill up fill
up fill up fill up
fill up fill

almonds

One by one
my senses leave
like children

with big plans
of their own.
One morning

I wake up
and my ears
have withdrawn

into my head.
Is it any better
beyond the body?

I watch a moth
wade into
the wrong light

and weep dust.
I take the moon
like a lozenge.

It drops into the
wash of my gut.
Who goes there?

candle

after Robert Lax

slow
light
on

a
fam
ily

of
str
ings

priorities

It was early evening and I was
on the porch with
a bottle of beer
and a book in my lap
and there was a hummingbird
feeding and
a tall pine was
rocking in the late summer breeze
and Pavarotti's voice was
coming through the speakers
just beyond the screen door
and I asked myself
If I could live with only
one of these things
for the rest of my small existence
which would it be?
and I sat there
thinking
for a few minutes
and couldn't come up with
an answer
but if I had to now
it would be the pine
rocking in the late summer breeze.

echo

> The tree beyond
> the window grows very large
> in my heart.

creatures

I stumble out
of bed into sweatpants and
socks and slippers.

Before I read
the news, I boil water
to make coffee.

So many concerns
for my little body to
handle right now.

My nose leaks
and so does the rest
of me, differently.

I just want
to be ready when the
light comes in.

To be ready
when the hinges and windows
start to talk.

The world speaks
and sometimes each of us
is only ever

quiet enough to
hear it in the night,
lost and found.

We sleep and
sounds wander the room on
soft animal feet.

Do you hear
the raccoons? They are a
horde of pirates

under the sill,
giggling about apples and trash
in the gravel.

A black bear
lumbers through the alley and
the raccoons scatter.

exceptional

The poet says yes
to all things

except
White Claw.

quiet

I picture Beethoven
hunched over his piano in
ecstasy, whispering through

a loud arpeggio
of thundering bass notes: *"Ist
es nicht schön?"*

"My dear friend,"
I say to him, "it
is unbearably loud."

"I am not
yet fully awake," he replies.
I take him

by the arm
to the bucket of water
just big enough

for his head
and say "Ludwig, this cannot
be the way."

He doesn't hear.
He points to the water
and says: "Listen"

childhood

She tells me to listen
while she reads
from a book.

She reads and she
moves her lips
all different.

I cannot understand
the what behind
the words

but I love them the
same I think be-
cause of her.

When utterly the quirk
shines on a lush
tongue I'm

all heels in the back
seat wondering
like wheels

what the space be-
tween me and
she really is.

diana

When there is no other light
It's like learning to swim

This is where you came from
And now you are here

I am beginning to get it
The mother in us all

Opens her legs to the sun
Soaks her heart in silence

Opens her mouth and sings
To the children of the night

All the stars and their smiles
And cries in the deep

  goose

duck duck duck
duck duck duck duck duck
duck duck duck

daughter

for B

A late morning
summer chill
sweeps 'round
the cafe

absent-
mindedly
ruffling
my cowlick.

Yes, I am
wearing shorts
and
a sweater.

Yes, we are
several years
into the third
millennium

since
the west
recognized
a prophet.

I was beginning
to lose hope
when I saw
the baby

in that
pickup truck
chewing
the steering wheel.

Dad leans forward
and kisses
the back of
her head.

birthday

Do you know
what your mother said
the moment before
you were born?
She said, in no
uncertain terms,
Get out of here!

vocabulary

It comes from the base of
the back of my
neck. A brittle unit

of darkness.
Belongs to me like
a building belongs to this Earth.

We forget. Do
strange and beautiful things
to remember

all that we are
against all that we
could have been.

poem

      in lieu of stepping out for a smoke
      in lieu of looking through old photos
      in lieu of staring at my lips in the bathroom
            mirror
      in lieu of listening to God in the shower
      in lieu of scaling my spine all the way out to
            the nub of my shrunken lemur tail
      in lieu of dipping two fingers into a vat of
            lemon water
      in lieu of watching who I have been blossom
            into who I cannot help but be
      in lieu of breathing like a fish on the floor

speech

Out of fear
of forgetting how to feel

behind the stony
teeth it stirs—

the wind of a word
in the lungs.

dont kill joe

www.ingramcontent.com/pod-product-compliance
Lightning Source LLC
Chambersburg PA
CBHW030535080526
44585CB00014B/957